MISSIONARIES
TO MATCH OUR MESSAGE

MISSIONARIES
To Match Our Message

Ezra Taft Benson

Bookcraft
Salt Lake City, Utah

Library of Congress Catalog Card Number: 90–85127

ISBN 0–88494–779–3

6th Printing, 1993

Printed in the United States of America

Contents

Contents

Preface

Today the Church needs missionaries as never before! We are required to carry the gospel of Jesus Christ to every nation of the world. The Lord commanded it in these words: "Send forth the elders of my church unto the nations which are afar off; unto the islands of the sea; send forth unto foreign lands; call upon all nations, first upon the Gentiles, and then upon the Jews" (D&C 133:8).

The Prophet Joseph Smith declared, "After all that has been said, [our] greatest and most important duty is to preach the Gospel" (*Teachings of the Prophet Joseph Smith*, sel. Joseph Fielding Smith [Salt Lake City: Deseret Book Co., 1938], p. 113).

I feel very deeply about missionary service in the kingdom. I pray that you will understand the yearnings of my heart.

Introduction:
The Urgent Need
to Serve

Many of our young men have not yet decided to give two years of service to the Lord. While you reap the benefits of a prosperity unprecedented in the history of mankind, do you ever think that one of the reasons why the Lord sent you to earth under such favorable circumstances is that you could use your talents, education, and money to bless others with the gospel?

✦✦✦

Not only should a mission be regarded as a priesthood duty, but every young man should look forward to this experience with great joy and anticipation.

What a privilege—what a sacred privilege—to serve the Lord full time for two years with all your heart, might, mind, and strength!

Young men, look forward to full-time missionary service. Show your love and commitment to the Lord by responding to His call to serve. Know that the real purpose in going into the mission field is to bring souls unto Christ, to teach and baptize our Heavenly Father's children so that you may rejoice with them in the kingdom of our Father (see D&C 18:15).

Remember, young women, you may also have the opportunity to serve a full-time mission. I am grateful my own eternal companion served a mission in Hawaii before we were married in the Salt Lake Temple, and I am pleased that I have had granddaughters serve full-time missions. Some of our finest missionaries are young sisters.

We urge couples to seriously consider serving a full-time mission. Many couples have provided distinguished service and stability to various missions in the Church.

We need increasing numbers of senior Church members in missionary service. Where health and means make it possible, we call upon hundreds more of our couples to set their lives and affairs in order and to go on missions. How we need you in the mission field! You are able to perform missionary service in ways that our younger missionaries cannot.

Most senior couples who go are strengthened and revitalized by missionary service. Through this holy avenue of service, many are sanctified and feel the joy of bringing others to the knowledge of the fulness of the gospel of Jesus Christ.

Preparing for a Successful Mission

Prepare Early and Well

Prepare well for a mission all your life, not just six months or a year before you go.

We love all of our missionaries who are serving the Lord full time in the mission field. But there is a difference in missionaries. Some are better prepared to serve the Lord the first month in the mission field than some who are returning home after twenty-four months.

✦✦✦

We want young men entering the mission field who can enter "on the run," who have the faith, born of personal righteousness and clean living, that they can have a great and productive mission.

Give me a young man who has kept himself morally clean and has faithfully attended his Church meetings. Give me a young man who has magnified his priesthood and has earned the Duty to God Award. Give me a young man who is a seminary graduate and has a burning testimony of the Book of Mormon. Give me such a young man, and I will give you a young man who can perform miracles for the Lord in the mission field and throughout his life.

Keep Yourself
Morally Clean

A vital ingredient in preparation for your mission is to always live a clean life. We want morally clean young men in the mission field. We want you to live the clean life all of your life. We want the morally clean life to be your way of life.

Yes, one can repent of moral transgression. The miracle of forgiveness is real, and true repentance is accepted of the Lord. But it is not pleasing to the Lord prior to a mission, or at any time, to sow one's wild oats, to engage in sexual transgression of any nature, and then to expect that planned confession and quick repentance will satisfy the Lord.

President Spencer W. Kimball was emphatic on this point. In his marvelous book *The Miracle of Forgiveness* he stated: "That man who resists temptation and lives without sin is far better off than the man who has fallen, no matter how repentant the latter may be. . . . How much better it is never to have committed the sin!" (Salt Lake City: Bookcraft, 1969, p. 357.)

Some young men, because of transgression, say they are not interested in serving a mission. The real reason for their reluctance, of course, is feelings of unworthiness. If any such young man will go to his bishop, confide to him his problem, and sincerely repent, he may yet fill an honorable mission. We, your Brethren, sincerely invite you to prepare. Prepare now to serve the Lord. Prepare yourself physically, morally, spiritually, and emotionally. Visit with your bishop. Tell him your desires. Confide your problems. Seek his counsel. Then pray to your Heavenly Father about this important decision in your life.

Prepare Yourself Physically, Mentally, Socially, and Spiritually

Prepare yourselves physically. A two-year mission today requires good physical health. It requires that you keep your body clean. In your early teenage years, when temptations come to you to take things into your body which are unsuitable, have the courage to resist. Live the Word of Wisdom—no smoking, no drinking of any alcoholic beverages, and no drugs. Keep your body pure—a pure vessel for the Lord.

Stay morally clean. This means that you keep a clean mind. Your thoughts will determine your actions, and so they must be controlled. It's difficult to control those thoughts if you submit yourself to temptation. So, you will have to carefully select your reading material, the movies you see, and the other forms of entertainment in order to have good thoughts rather than unwholesome desires.

Prepare yourselves mentally. A mission requires a great deal of mental preparation. You must memorize missionary discussions, memorize scriptures, and ofttimes learn a new language. The discipline to do this is learned in your early years.

Establish now the practice of reading the scriptures ten to fifteen minutes each day. If you do so, by the time you reach the mission field you will have read all four of the standard works. I urge you to read particularly the Book of Mormon so that you can testify of its truthfulness as the Lord has directed.

Prepare yourselves socially. A mission requires that you get along with others. You must get along with your companion, who is with you twenty-four hours a day. You must learn to meet people and be gracious and practice good manners. One of the greatest assets that a person can have in life is the ability to make friends. When you make a friend of a person, you can teach him the gospel.

Prepare yourselves spiritually. A spiritual person obeys all the Lord's commandments. He prays to our Heavenly Father, and he gives service to others.

Yes, young men, prepare now. Prepare yourselves physically, mentally, socially, and spiritually. Always be obedient to authority. Start a savings account for your mission if you haven't done so already. Pay your tithing, and seek a testimony of the gospel through study and prayer.

Gain a Burning Testimony

You must have a burning testimony of the divinity of this work if you are going to succeed in the mission field. Your first obligation is to get that testimony through prayer, through fasting, through meditation, through study, through appealing to the Lord to give you the testimony, through responding to calls when they come to you. You must have a testimony of the divinity of this work. You must know that God lives; that Jesus is the Christ, the Redeemer of the world; that Joseph Smith is a prophet of God; that the priesthood and authority of our Heavenly Father is here; and that you bear that priesthood and have the authority to represent Him in the world.

Know and Love
the Book of Mormon

Reading the Book of Mormon is one of the greatest persuaders to get men on missions. We need more missionaries. But we also need better-prepared missionaries coming out of wards and branches and homes where they know and love the Book of Mormon. A great challenge and day of preparation is at hand for missionaries to meet and teach with the Book of Mormon. We need missionaries to match our message.

❧❧❧

Young men, the Book of Mormon will change your life. It will fortify you against the evils of our day. It will bring a spirituality into your life that no other book will. It will be the most important book you will read in preparation for a mission and for life. A young man who knows and loves the Book of Mormon, who has read it several times, who has an abiding testimony of its truthfulness, and who applies its teachings will be able to stand against the wiles of the devil and will be a mighty tool in the hands of the Lord.

Serving a Successful Mission

.

Follow the Example of Great Missionaries

The Book of Mormon tells us about some of the most successful missionaries who have ever gone forth to preach the gospel. Four of these were the sons of Mosiah, named Ammon, Aaron, Omner, and Himni. They were men of God and had prepared themselves spiritually to do the work. From them we have a great example to follow. You will remember that they were converted at the same time Alma the Younger was and that then they repented of their sins and went on missions to the Lamanites.

In the book of Alma these missionaries and their success are described in the following words: "They had waxed strong in the knowledge of the truth; for they were men of a sound understanding and they had searched the scriptures diligently, that they might know the word of God. But this is not all; they had given themselves to much prayer, and fasting." And here are the results of their preparations: "Therefore they had the spirit of prophecy, and the spirit of revelation, and when they taught, they taught with power and authority of God." (Alma 17:2–3.)

There are great verses of scripture that have particular application to missionary work. Alma 26:22 is an example of one of the greatest. Here Ammon is rejoicing in the success the Lord has blessed him with in his missionary work among the Lamanites. And then he gives four keys for missionaries to use in bringing thousands of souls to repentance.

He is speaking directly to missionaries when he says: "Yea, he that repenteth and exerciseth faith, and bringeth forth good works, and prayeth continually without ceasing—unto such it is given to know the mysteries of God; yea, unto such it shall be given to reveal things which never have been revealed; yea, and it shall be given unto such to bring thousands of souls to repentance, even as it has been given unto us to bring these our brethren to repentance." What a marvelous verse of scripture!

First, Ammon says that a missionary should be certain that his personal life is in order, keeping his thoughts clean, not going after the lusts of his eyes, being obedient to all mission rules.

Second, Ammon says that a missionary should exercise faith, believing that he can do great things for the Lord, that he can achieve his personal goals, that he can find golden families and teach them with the Spirit and baptize them. "If thou canst believe, all things are possible to him that believeth" (Mark 9:23). "I can do all things through Christ which strengtheneth me" (Philippians 4:13). These scriptures on faith should be imbedded into every missionary's mind and heart.

Third, Ammon challenges missionaries to work diligently. Missionary work is *not* easy. It is the most demanding, the most compelling, the most exhausting, and yet, with it all, the most happy and joyful work in all the world.

But it requires work. If missionaries really work, they will get the Spirit. If they get the Spirit, they will teach by the Spirit. And if they teach by the Spirit, they will be instruments in the hands of the Lord in bringing thousands of souls unto Him.

Fourth, Ammon tells missionaries that they should pray without ceasing. They should pour out their hearts to the Lord and plead to the Lord for their investigators. The "fervent prayer of a righteous man availeth much" (James 5:16).

Yes, Ammon urges missionaries to live righteously, to exercise faith, to work hard, and to pray continually. Then they will receive personal revelation in their missionary work, which will allow them to bring a harvest of souls into the Church. These are true principles.

Be Obedient

Obedience is the first law of heaven. Missionaries, be obedient, not because you have to but because you want to. You can, in a sense, bind the Lord with cords of righteousness if you are obedient, if you are faithful, if you keep the mission rules. By so doing you will be blessed in achieving your righteous goals. (See D&C 82:10.)

Obedience brings perfection. Even the Savior Himself learned this eternal principle: "Though he were a Son, yet learned he obedience by the things which he suffered" (Hebrews 5:8). Some missionaries may suffer a bit as they learn this principle, as they bend their will to the will of the Lord. But, oh, what blessings follow! There is nothing like a faithful, humble sister or elder who has learned the principle of obedience. How such missionaries can be used by the Lord!

The white *Missionary Handbook* published by the First Presidency should be given great emphasis. Personally I would recommend that missionaries and their companions read from the handbook daily.

Have Faith

Develop simple but powerful faith—the kind of faith that performs miracles for the Lord in the mission field.

First and foremost have faith in the Lord Jesus Christ, that He is the head of the Church, that He is directing the work, and that His purposes will be accomplished on your mission.

Doubt not, fear not. If you are true to your calling, your faith will be realized in accomplishing specific righteous goals.

Remember the words of Ammon: "I know that I am nothing; as to my strength I am weak; therefore I will not boast of myself, but I will boast of my God, for in his strength I can do all things" (Alma 26:12).

Know that to the extent you exercise faith in Christ you will perform miracles in the mission field and bring souls unto Him.

Work Hard

If you want to keep the Spirit, to love your mission and not be homesick, you must work.

There is no greater exhilaration or satisfaction than to know, after a hard day of work, that you have done your best.

I have often said that one of the greatest secrets of missionary work is work! If a missionary works, he will get the Spirit; if he gets the Spirit, he will teach by the Spirit; and if he teaches by the Spirit, he will touch the hearts of the people and he will be happy. There will be no homesickness, no worrying about families—for all time and talents and interest will be centered on the work of the ministry. Work, work, work—there is no satisfactory substitute, especially in missionary work.

The busy missionary is the happy missionary. I cannot recall a missionary ever going astray who was really active and busy. Occasionally we have missionaries who make mistakes. It usually starts when they become idle, when they stay in their lodgings when they ought to be out with the people. Occasionally you will find a missionary who is looking for excuses not to go out—who can look out the window and see a storm coming when there isn't any, who can see rain when it isn't raining. The important thing is to get out with the people, to keep active, to be devoted. Do not sleep longer than is needful. The same Lord who gave the Word of Wisdom in the 89th section of the Doctrine and Covenants also gave that instruction in the 88th section, and it is just as binding as the counsel that you are not to use tobacco or alcoholic beverages. So, cease from all light-mindedness, cease to sleep longer than is needful, and retire to your bed early (see D&C 88:121, 124). You will be more effective, you will do more work, you will be happier, and you will have better health.

We want missionaries who arise early every day, who study diligently, who go tracting with the purpose of finding golden contacts, who challenge and teach with the Spirit, who return home every evening "tired in the Lord," and who literally have their bodies renewed daily in His service.

It is so important that you lose yourselves in this work, that you don't worry about "What is it going to do for me?" You are not out in the world with self-improvement as the major objective, but you can't help getting a maximum amount of self-improvement if you lose yourself in the work of the Lord. I don't know of any better preparation for life than two years of devoted, unselfish service as a missionary.

Pray Fervently

Missionaries, know the power of prayer. Pray to find the honest in heart on a given day, in a given hour. Pray over your individual investigators; pray for specific direction as you teach by the Spirit; pray to reach your righteous goals; pray for convert baptisms in a specific way, humbly petitioning the Lord for His help, for His direction.

❧

Brethren and sisters, we cannot do this work alone. This is His work. This is His gospel. We must have His help. Plead for it, live for it, pour out your soul to the Lord to receive it.

"The effectual fervent prayer of a righteous man availeth much" (James 5:16).

"Be thou humble; and the Lord thy God shall lead thee by the hand, and give thee answer to thy prayers" (D&C 112:10).

And remember the words of the Savior as recorded in 3 Nephi: "Whatsoever ye shall ask the Father in my name, which is right, believing that ye shall receive, behold it shall be given unto you" (18:20). You should live by that verse of scripture.

Remember, you are never alone in this work. He is always there. Reach out for His infinite help. Prayer is a principle of spiritual power and will be forever.

Don't Get Discouraged

As missionaries you must not allow yourselves to become discouraged. Missionary work brings joy, optimism, and happiness. Don't give Satan an opportunity to discourage you.

🙟

Missionary work is not easy work, and Satan will take every opportunity to discourage a missionary. When these moments come, the yoke you are called to bear may seem heavy and unbearable.

The Lord has given us a key by which we can overcome discouragement. Our Savior extended an invitation to us when He said: "Come unto me, all ye that labour and are heavy laden, and I will give you rest. Take my yoke upon you, and learn of me; for I am meek and lowly in heart: and ye shall find rest unto your souls. For my yoke is easy, and my burden is light." (Matthew 11:28–30.)

In olden days the purpose of a yoke was to get oxen to pull evenly together in a united effort. In a sense our Savior has a load to pull, a cause to move forward. He has asked us to become yoked with Him to help move His gospel forward unto all those who will accept. "My yoke is easy, and my burden is light."

Your work will be light, or easy, to bear—no matter how difficult it becomes—if the burden you bear is the work of Jesus Christ. As you approach your work in this spirit you will be able to see all problems as challenges and not as stumbling blocks. And most important of all, you will increase in spirituality.

Don't worry about being successful. You are going to be successful—there is no doubt about it. The Lord has sent you out into the field at the time of harvest. He does not expect you to fail. He has called no one to this work to fail. He expects us to succeed.

Don't Aspire
to Positions

The principle of not aspiring to positions in the mission field is taught well in Mark 9:34–35 and Matthew 23:11–12. Missionaries should be taught that it doesn't matter where they serve, but how. Position doesn't save anyone, but faithfulness does. Aspiring to positions of responsibility can destroy the spirit of the mission as well as the spirit of a missionary.

I had been discussing this point with a group of missionaries in Innsbruck, Austria, back in 1965, when at the end of a meeting one of the fine missionaries handed me a little card on which I found the following:

My Little Place

"Father, where shall I work today?"
And my love flowed warm and free.

Then He pointed me out a tiny spot
    And said, "Tend that for me."
I answered quickly, "Oh no, not that!
    Why, no one would ever see,
No matter how well my work was done;
    Not that little place for me."
And the words He spoke, they were not stern,
    He answered me tenderly,
"Ah, little one, search that heart of thine:
    Art thou working for them or me?
Nazareth was a little place,
    And so was Galilee."

We'll all be expected to stand before the Lord at the last day. John, on the Isle of Patmos, said that he "saw the dead, small and great, stand before God; and the books were opened: and another book was opened, which is the book of life: and the dead were judged out of those things which were written in the books" (Revelation 20:12).

I have a feeling that on that important day the question will not be so much "What office did you hold?" The real question will be "Did you serve me with all your heart, might, mind, and strength?" God bless us that we may serve so that we will never have any serious regrets, that we will know we have been magnified even beyond our natural talents.

Be Humble

The Lord has said, "No one can assist in this work except he shall be humble and full of love" (D&C 12:8). But humility does not mean weakness. It does not mean timidity. It does not mean fear. A man can be humble and fearless. A man can be humble and courageous. Humility means a recognition of our dependence upon a higher power, of our need for the Lord's support in His work.

Speaking to the early elders of the Church the Lord said: "But with some I am not well pleased, for they will not open their mouths, but they hide the talent which I have given unto them, because of the fear of man. Wo unto such, for mine anger is kindled against them." (D&C 60:2.)

That is pretty plain, isn't it? Sometimes we have among our missionaries those who are afraid because of the fear of man, and if you permit yourselves to get that spirit of fear, the adversary will back you up. He will support you. He will encourage you in it until you get to the point where you are afraid to exercise your authority and to bear testimony regarding this message. Remember the promise made: "And they shall go forth and none shall stay them, for I the Lord have commanded them" (D&C 1:5). There is no place for fear. There is no place for discouragement, because you can't fail in this work if you do your part. There is no place for timidity or hesitancy. Humility, yes, but you can be humble and courageous and fearless and effective, all at the same time.

Love the People

You must develop a love for the people among whom you labor in the mission field. Your hearts must go out to them in pure love of the gospel, in a desire to lift them, to build them up, to point them to a higher, finer life and, eventually, to exaltation in the celestial kingdom of God. Emphasize the fine qualities of the people you are to teach. Love the people as children of God, whom the Lord loves.

The Prophet Joseph Smith taught: "God does not look on sin with allowance, but when men have sinned, there must be allowance made for them" (*Teachings of the Prophet Joseph Smith,* sel. Joseph Fielding Smith [Salt Lake City: Deseret Book Co., 1938], pp. 240–41). That is another way of saying God loves the sinner but condemns the sin.

You will not be an effective missionary until you learn to have sympathy for all of our Father's children, until you learn to love them. People can feel when love is extended to them. Many yearn for it. When you sympathize with their feelings, they in turn will reciprocate goodwill to you. You will have made a friend. As the Prophet Joseph Smith taught, "Whom can I teach but my friends?" Yes, love the people.

Also love your companion and overlook his shortcomings. Contention between missionary companions drives out the Spirit—love fosters it.

Love the area in which you are laboring, and do not speak disparagingly of it. With Christlike love, love the members of the Church in your area, and appreciate what they do to support missionary work.

And truly love your investigators into the waters of baptism. We should challenge investigators to baptism with true love for them, desiring with all of our hearts to bring them salvation and exaltation. There is no greater love than the love for souls.

Use the Book of Mormon

The Book of Mormon must become the center of our personal study, our preaching, and our missionary work. We are not yet doing all that the Lord would have us do. Of this we must repent. The Book of Mormon must be the heart of our missionary work in every mission of the Church.

🙰

The Book of Mormon is for both member and nonmember. Combined with the Spirit of the Lord, the Book of Mormon is the greatest single tool which God has given us to convert the world. If we are to have the harvest of souls, we must use the instrument which God has designed for that task—the Book of Mormon.

Anyone who has diligently sought to know the doctrines and teachings of the Book of Mormon and has used it conscientiously in missionary work knows within his soul that this is the instrument which God has given to the missionaries to convince the Jew and Gentile and Lamanite of the truthfulness of our message.

Missionaries should read daily from the Book of Mormon. There is a spiritual power in the Book of Mormon which makes it unique among all other scriptures. Indeed, as the Prophet Joseph Smith declared, "a man [will] get nearer to God by abiding by its precepts, than by any other book" (Book of Mormon Introduction, 1981 edition). Every missionary needs the power of the Book of Mormon to continue to bring conversion to his own soul and to increase his own spirituality. With that power missionaries should use the Book of Mormon as the heart of their proselyting work and as the great converter.

We need missionaries to match our message. We need missionaries who really know and love the Book of Mormon, who have a burning testimony of its divinity, and who by the Spirit can challenge their investigators to read and ponder its pages, knowing with complete assurance that the Lord will manifest the truth of the Book of Mormon to them by the power of the Holy Ghost.

To be effective, a missionary who is inspired by the Spirit of the Lord must be led by that Spirit to choose the proper approach. We must not forget that the Lord Himself provided the Book of Mormon as His chief witness. The Book of Mormon is still our most powerful missionary tool. Let's use it.

Accelerate Member-Missionary Work

Our members need to understand their responsibility to do missionary work and then do it. Missionaries need to help them fulfill their missionary responsibility. I fully endorse the words of President Spencer W. Kimball: "Do we really believe in revelation? Then why cannot we accept fully as the revealed word of God the revelation of the Prophet-President David O. McKay, wherein he brought to the Church and to the world this valuable Church slogan, 'Every member a missionary'? . . .

"How else could the Lord expect to perform His work except through the Saints who have covenanted to serve Him? You and I have made such a covenant. Will we honor our sacred covenant?" (Regional Representatives' seminar, 30 September 1977.)

Member-missionary work is the key to the future growth of the Church. We must, therefore, involve the members of the Church more effectively in missionary work.

This can be done in an organized and effective manner. The key to member-missionary work is *correlation* between full-time missionaries and the stakes and wards in which full-time missionaries serve.

Correlation with the wards and stakes in having one interrelated missionary program is vital to the success of full-time and stake missionary work. This whole area of priesthood-missionary correlation is so vital to the success of missionary work that I cannot speak too strongly about it.

Missionary work cannot be effectively handled independent of the stakes and wards or with poor correlation. Challenge the members to do their missionary work, but challenge them with love and not criticism. Do it by motivating them, not by berating them.

Let the members know that the Lord will sustain them in their missionary responsibility if they just have the faith to try. Quote to them Acts 18:9–10: "Be not afraid, but speak, and hold not thy peace: for I am with thee, and no man shall set on thee to hurt thee: for I have much people in this city." Share with them the joy they will experience by finding and fellowshipping friends and neighbors for you to teach.

I promise you that you will more than double your convert baptisms if full-time missionaries and members and leaders in the stakes and wards correlate missionary work as they should and work together in harmony. I issue you that challenge!

I promise you that you will more than double your convert baptisms if full-time missionaries and members and leaders in the stakes and wards correlate missionary work as they should and work together in harmony. I issue you that challenge!

Too many missionaries are neutralized, and occasionally lost, because of oversolicitous members, member sisters who "mother" the missionaries, and socializing occurring between missionaries and members. Because of the importance of members and missionaries working effectively together on the member-missionary program, it is vital that missionaries maintain the proper missionary image and have the reputation of being great proselyting elders and not just "good guys." The greatest help members can be to a missionary is not to feed him, but to give him names of their friends so he can teach them with the Spirit in their homes and challenge them with the wonderful members helping to fellowship.

Set Personal Goals

Missionaries should know the principles of goal setting. For over a decade our beloved President Spencer W. Kimball taught the Church, and particularly our missionaries, the importance of setting goals. He declared: "I feel that we must use a goal program and let every missionary make his own goal" (Regional Representatives' seminar, 3 October 1974). "We do believe in setting goals. . . . Our most important goal is to bring the gospel to all people. We must convert more people. We must find ways and means." (Regional Representatives' seminar, 3 April 1975.)

The missionary is entitled to inspiration in choosing his personal goals; and when he has sought the Lord through prayer and meditation, he will be motivated best by those goals he selects himself and commits himself to attain.

Missionaries should have a standard of performance or excellence to which they ascribe and to which they commit. Missionaries should take pride in being in "the best mission in the Church" (for them) and being "missionaries of excellence."

Increase Convert Baptisms

Your purpose for being in the mission field is to save souls, to baptize converts, to bring converted families into the Lord's church. I ask you to give particular attention to scriptures which explain your holy calling—such as Doctrine and Covenants sections 4, 11, 15, 16, and 18, and the Book of Mormon.

&&&

It is a time of harvest in your mission field and not a time of gleaning, and if you are true and faithful you will literally be instruments in the hands of the Lord in bringing souls unto Him. Remember the Apostle Paul's statement that in the conversion process some missionaries will plant, some will water, and some will baptize. We are *not* concerned with who gets the credit for the baptisms because "God [gives] the increase." (1 Corinthians 3:6.) All we are concerned about is that you have a burning desire to bring souls unto Him.

Feel the spirit of the modern-day challenging and testifying missionary who prays every morning, "Lead me this day to a family, that I can fulfill my purpose. I will testify unto them by thy power without hesitancy or fear, and will lead them by the power of the Spirit to baptism into thy kingdom."

Receive the Joy

You are in the mission field to testify of the greatest event which has transpired in this world since the resurrection of the Master—the coming of God the Father and His Son, Jesus Christ, to the boy prophet. You are sent out to testify of a new volume of scripture—a new witness for Christ. May God bless you to testify effectively, to bear a strong testimony to the truthfulness of this glorious message.

I pray your joy will be full and that, like Ammon of old, you will be able to say: "I do not boast in my own strength, nor in my own wisdom; but behold, my joy is full, yea, my heart is brim with joy, and I will rejoice in my God. Yea, I know that I am nothing; as to my strength I am weak; therefore I will not boast of myself, but I will boast of my God, for in his strength I can do all things; yea, behold, many mighty miracles we have wrought in this land, for which we will praise his name forever." (Alma 26:11–12.)

Know of the joy that will fill your heart when you have taught an investigator with love and with the Spirit, when you have given the baptismal challenge, and then when you have seen a wonderful family enter into the waters of baptism.

Missionaries, labor with all your heart, might, mind, and strength—for that is where the joy is—to go home at the end of each day "tired in the Lord" to be renewed by the Lord in the morning.

Appendix

Sources for the selections in this volume are as follows:

"The Book of Mormon Is the Word of God." *Ensign* 18 (January 1988): 3–5.

Come, Listen to a Prophet's Voice. Salt Lake City: Deseret Book Co., 1990.

Come unto Christ. Salt Lake City: Deseret Book Co., 1983.

God, Family, Country. Salt Lake City: Deseret Book Co., 1974.

"Keys to Successful Member–Missionary Work." *Ensign* 20 (September 1990): 2–7.

"My Challenge to Mission Presidents." Address delivered at mission presidents' seminar, 25 June 1986, Provo, Utah.

"A New Witness for Christ." *Ensign* 14 (November 1984): 6–8.

"Preparing Yourselves for Missionary Service." *Ensign* 15 (May 1985): 36–37.

"Principles for Performing Miracles in Missionary Work." Address delivered at mission presidents' seminar, 23 June 1987, Provo, Utah.

The Teachings of Ezra Taft Benson. Salt Lake City: Bookcraft, 1988.

"This Is a Day of Sacrifice." *Ensign* 9 (May 1979): 32–34.

"To the Elderly in the Church." *Ensign* 19 (November 1989): 4–8.

"To 'the Rising Generation.' " *New Era* 16 (June 1986): 4–8.

"To the Single Adult Brethren of the Church." *Ensign* 18 (May 1988): 51–53.

"To the Young Women of the Church." *Ensign* 16 (November 1986): 81–85.

"To the 'Youth of the Noble Birthright.' " *Ensign* 16 (May 1986): 43–46.

A Witness and a Warning. Salt Lake City: Deseret Book Co., 1988.

"Youth—Promise for the Future." Address delivered at Ricks College devotional, 12 March 1985, Rexburg, Idaho.